I'm shy

WAYLAND

Your Feelings

I'm bored   I'm shy
I'm lonely   I'm happy
I'm worried   I feel bullied
It's not fair   I'm special

First published in 1998 by
Wayland Publishers Ltd
61 Western Road, Hove
East Sussex BN3 1JD, England

 Find out about how this book is relevant to the National Literacy Strategy on page 31.

find Wayland on the Internet at http://www.wayland.co.uk

Series editor: Alex Woolf
Designer: Malcolm Walker

British Library Cataloguing in Publication Data

Bryant-Mole, Karen
    I'm shy. - (Your feelings)
    1.Bashfulness - Pictorial works - Juvenile literature
    I.Title
    155.4'18'232

ISBN 0 7502 2335 9

Typeset by Malcolm Walker
Colour Separation by P&W Graphics, Singapore
Printed and bound in Italy by G. Canale & C.S.p.A., Turin

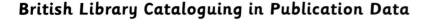

I'm shy

Written by Karen Bryant-Mole

Illustrated by Mike Gordon

WAYLAND

When I'm feeling shy, I feel like ...

a flower that doesn't want to open ...

a baby chick hiding under its mother's wing ...

a quiet triangle in a loud orchestra.

When I'm feeling shy ...
my face goes red ...

my legs and tummy feel wobbly.

When I'm feeling shy ...

sometimes I am very quiet ...

sometimes I giggle.
But it isn't a happy sort of giggle.
It's a worried sort of giggle.

9

When the teacher asks me a question,
I feel shy.

I'm worried that I might get the answer wrong or say something silly.
Everyone might laugh at me.

When I'm in a play at school, I feel shy.

But when everyone claps, I feel quite proud of myself.

When I go to parties, I sometimes feel shy. I don't want to play the party games.

But, after a while, I stop feeling quite so shy. When I see how much fun my friends are having, I join in too.

When I visit great-aunt Maud, I feel shy.

But I stop feeling shy when she asks me if I would like to help her make some cakes for tea.

Sometimes grown-ups feel shy too.

My mum felt shy when she went to a party and didn't know anyone else there.

My dad says he felt shy
on his wedding day
because he knew everyone
would be looking at him
and my mum.

Grown-ups sometimes feel shy when they meet important or famous people.

23

When I'm feeling shy, I wish I
were a magician ...

then I could make
myself invisible.

When I'm feeling shy it helps if people smile at me.

Perhaps you know someone who sometimes feels shy.

What could
you do to help?

Notes for parents and teachers

This book can be read either with individual children or with a group of children. Ask the children to look again at the images on pages 4 and 5 and say which image best matches the way they feel when they are feeling shy. See if children can come up with other images that illustrate how they feel. This can be facilitated by encouraging children to start with the phrase, 'I'm as shy as ...'.

Different children feel shy in different situations. Children could discuss which situations make them feel shy and then think about what it is that makes them feel shy. It might be that they feel that they are going to be asked to do something that they can't, that they are going to look silly in front of other people or just that they don't want to draw attention to themselves.

Feelings of shyness are often linked to other feelings such as embarrassment, worry, fear or nervousness. Look back through the situations described in the book and see if the children can decide which emotions, if any, are being displayed in addition to shyness.

Discuss other words relating to shyness, such as 'bashful' and 'timid'. Describe being shy as part of what makes up someone's character. Some children only feel shy some of the time.

Other children feel shy most of the time. Children could think of words that describe other facets of their character, such as 'noisy', 'messy' and 'cheerful'. They could imagine that they were writing to a pen pal, describing their own character. Within a classroom situation, children could write anonymous descriptions of their character, which could be read out and the class invited to guess who was being described.

Children could think of ways to help someone overcome his or her shyness, such as asking a shy child to join in with their games, by not being loud or rough, by being friendly or by saying that they like something the child has done.

Use this book for teaching literacy

This book can help in you in the literacy hour in the following ways:

- ✓ Children can write simple stories linked to personal experience, using the language of the text in this book as a model for their own writing. (Year 1, Term 3: Non-fiction writing composition)

- ✓ The repeated use of phrases such as 'When I'm feeling shy ...' helps with word recognition and spelling. (Year 2: Word recognition and graphic knowledge)

- ✓ Use of speech bubbles and enlarged print shows different ways of presenting texts (Year 2, Term 2: Sentence construction and punctuation)

Books to read

The Snow Fairy and the Spaceman by Catherine Anholt (Heinemann, 1990; paperback edition by Mammoth). A little boy is at a birthday party, feeling very shy. He goes outside to get away from everyone. An accident happens and he runs to the rescue of the birthday girl. His confidence is restored and he stops feeling shy.

Poonam's Pets written by Andrew and Diana Davies, illustrated by Paul Dowling (Mammoth, 1992). A story about a small, shy girl called Poonam. When the class teacher suggests a pets' assembly the children bring in ordinary pets, such as cats and dogs. But when Poonam arrives everyone gets a big surprise and Poonam is never quite so shy again.

The Tooth Ball written by Philippa Pearce, illustrated by Helen Ganly (Andre Deutsch, 1987). This book tells the story of a boy called Timmy, who is too shy to make friends. However, a wish, together with a mysterious tooth ball, soon change all this.

Snuffles makes a Friend written by Mary Donavan, illustrated by Caroline Anstey (Walker Books, 1995). Snuffles enjoys having a house full of friends. When Percy moves in next door, Snuffles keeps on inviting him around but Percy always refuses. It turns out that Percy is shy and does not like meeting a lot of people at once. So he meets Snuffles' friends one at a time.